W9-CRJ-942

Tim Crosby

Visitors' Guide to Ancient Forests of Western Washington

By the Dittmar Family for The Wilderness Society

by the Dittmars: Ann, David, Jane, Tom, Judy and Steve

The Wilderness Society
1400 Eye Street, N.W. Washington, D.C. 20005 (202) 842 3400
Second printing 1990

Cover photograph by Tim Crosby. Dedication photograph by Ann Dittmar.
Design by Luci Goodman and Ginny Perkins. Illustrations by Jon Gardescu.
Distributed by The Mountaineers Books.

printed in the United States of America
ISBN 0-89886-247-7

Dedication

Dedicated to the ancient trees that have fallen and now nurture tall seedlings, in the hope that the natural cycle will be allowed to continue.

And to Stan Dittmar, who gave us so much to live for and so many skills to live with.

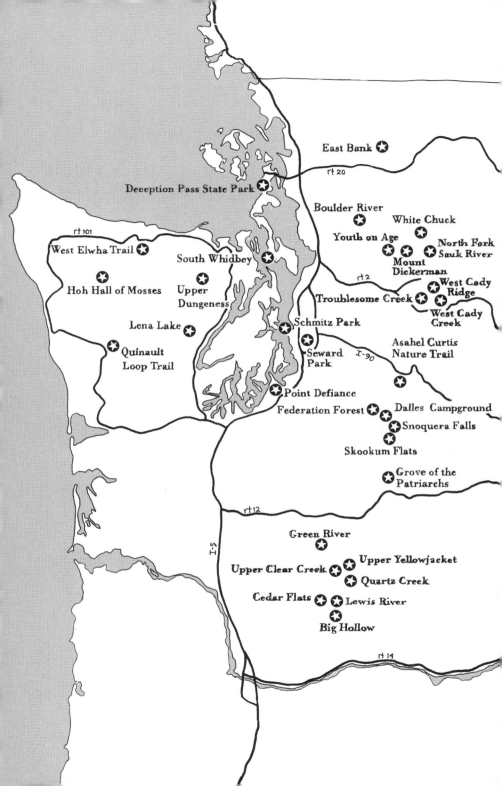

East Bank ✪

rt 20

Deception Pass State Park ✪

Boulder River
✪

White Chuck
✪

Youth on Age ✪

North Fork
✪ ✪ Sauk River

Mount
Dickerman

West Elwha Trail ✪

South Whidbey ✪

rt 101

West Cady
✪ Ridge

Hoh Hall of Mosses ✪

Upper
Dungeness ✪

Troublesome Creek ✪

West Cady
Creek

rt 2

Lena Lake ✪

Schmitz Park ✪

Asahel Curtis
Nature Trail

✪ Quinault
Loop Trail

✪
Seward
Park

I-90

✪

Point Defiance ✪

Federation Forest ✪ ✪ Dalles Campground

✪ Snoquera Falls

Skookum Flats ✪

✪ Grove of the
Patriarchs

rt 12

Green River
✪

Upper Clear Creek ✪ ✪ ✪ Upper Yellowjacket

✪ Quartz Creek

Cedar Flats ✪ ✪ Lewis River

✪
Big Hollow

I-5

rt 14

Table
of Contents

9 Foreword

11 Introduction

13 What is an Old-Growth Forest?

15 Olympic Peninsula

23 Northern Cascades

35 Central Cascades

41 Southern Cascades

51 Puget Sound Area

57 The Future of Ancient Forests

60 More Ancient Forest Areas

67 How to Identify Common Conifers

71 Additional Information

75 Bibliography

79 Acknowledgements

pacific jumping mouse

Peter Morrison

Foreword

After the last ice age the Pacific Northwest grew into endless forests of some of the world's most majestic trees. From time to time, patches would be killed by windstorm, fire or volcano but vast stretches remained primeval forest. Coastal northwest Indians traveled the waterways more than the land, because the tangled forest floor made passage difficult.

When pioneer settlers arrived, their first and most daunting task was clearing trees to conquer the wilderness. The hills of Seattle fed Henry Yesler's sawmill; Everett was founded by timber entrepreneurs; from harbors up and down the coast, pilings and lumber were shipped to San Francisco.

The power of humans to transform the landscape is dramatically evidenced by the need, after only 150 years of settlement, for a guidebook to help people find any virgin forest at all in the Evergreen State.

An initial glance at this book might lead one to think many examples survive of the original forest. Certainly, the places described here have big trees. But fragments should not be confused with a forest. Groves near populated areas are few and small. In some places only remnant large trees stand amid younger forest. To reach intact stands of ancient forest can require miles of driving dirt roads, sometimes then to be blocked by a logging operation barring the way. Of the original forest that remains today, much may soon be gone.

Most ancient forest still standing is managed by the U.S. Forest Service, and much of that is subject to logging. As can be seen most clearly from the air, Washington's canopy of forest is increasingly fragmented. If past patterns of timber sales and clearcuts continue, ancient forest may disappear except within official wilderness and parks. If that happens, the woods protected could be little more than tree museums.

All of us, indeed all the world, owe profound gratitude to the citizens and political leaders who protected forests in national, state and local parks and in the National Wilderness Preservation System. A very few large sections of forest will remain, subject only to changes of nature. But even wilderness areas specifically established to protect marvelous ancient forest, such as the Clearwater Wildernesses north of Mount Rainier, may not include the best of the contiguous forest giants. New steps must be taken to protect the ancient forest. We rightly decry destruction of tropical rainforests, but to date only 15% of the Amazon basin is gone while 87% of the old growth of the Northwest has been cut.

The Wilderness Society has long led the charge for the great forests of the Pacific Northwest. In 1936 its magazine championed "The Third Greatest American Tree," the Douglas-firs of the Olympic Peninsula. Recently The Society has published studies on Forest Service management plans in the Northwest, on the region's timber economy, and on the inventory of old growth actually remaining on national forests (see Bibliography). Working with many others we hope to inform all Americans of the plight of the Northwest's ancient forests. Working with Congress and government agencies we citizens must end the wholesale destruction of the magnificent heritage that is our ancient forests. We ask your help.

Jean C. Durning
Regional Director, The Wilderness Society

Introduction

This visitor's guide to ancient forests in western Washington invites you to take a stroll through our Northwest heritage and gather a sense of life as it was before the Space Needle and ferry boats, before airplanes and loggers.

Using this guide you can seek out the past, take a hike into history and pay your respects to the ancient forests. These few remaining stands were once part of one of the greatest natural ecosystems that ever evolved on our planet. Visit the old trees and come to an understanding of the complex yet delicate balance that has kept some of these giant trees alive for nearly 1,000 years. In the ancient forest you can absorb the wisdom of the ages while being sheltered from the frenzy of modern life.

Once you are deep inside the forest, stop for a spell and touch the spongy mosses, peer into the logs' crevices and smell the bark. Take a moment to sit and count the various shades of green and let the forest canopy shelter you from the sun or rain. Notice the crumbling log that gives life to the towering giants as well as the smallest of mushrooms and lichens. Lean back and gaze skyward to observe the canopy. Let yourself relax, breathe into the deep earth and out into the sky, becoming a part of the forest.

Use this guidebook to launch your own adventure to some of the last fragments of old growth while these treasures are still standing. Now is the time to visit and enjoy their beauty.

What to Take: Before heading out into the woods, you should be prepared. The sites listed in this book vary from paved and well-signed nature trails to dirt roads, trails and trackless backcountry. If you will be off the main-travelled ways, get a good map that shows all the roads and trails. You can get such maps from the Forest Service or from an outdoor sporting goods store.

For travel in more remote areas, check the weather conditions before heading out. Call the ranger station, better yet, stop by on your way to the area (ranger stations may be closed on weekends). Forest and park staff are always happy to provide you with information and to tell you about the current trail conditions.

The most important thing to remember is to use your common sense. After all, you are going on these trips to enjoy some of nature's oldest gifts. Spend the few minutes it takes to prepare before you reach your destination, so that you can give your full attention to the wonders of the woods. Hikers should take the "Ten Essentials" (see page 71). Nature can be unforgiving at times to people who are not properly prepared.

What to Leave: Leave the forests just as you entered them: natural and free of reminders of man and civilization. Leave only footprints and take with you only the memories of the sights, sounds and smells you experience in the wonderful world of ancient forests.

What is an Old-Growth Forest?

Old growth is a technical term for ancient virgin forests. An old-growth forest is more than just big trees; many factors are included in official definitions. For simplicity's sake, the following is an overview of the characteristics that will help you identify the ancient forests in western Washington:

An old-growth forest is a complex, diverse and highly evolved ecosystem. The centerpiece of the system is the trees. Old-growth forests have never been logged and the dominant trees that are still standing and growing are at least 200 years old — some are even 1000 years old. Many species and sizes of trees, some with broken tops, create uneven canopies, a multi-layered forest ceiling. Old-growth forests also have dead trees, still standing, that provide shelter for swifts and bats, and food for woodpeckers and lichens. And there are fallen giants, necessary to provide nutrients in the soil and to give life to seedlings which may someday become ancient trees. Also, old-growth forests have fallen trees in streams that give nutrients and energy to the waters, helping to support life from caddis flies to mighty salmon.

The lives of thousands of plants, animals and insects revolve around the life-cycle of the old-growth trees. One life gives life to others — multiple layers each dependent upon the other as the chain of life weaves an intricate web of survival. From bacteria and fungus spores on and under the ground to the northern flying squirrel and the spotted owl high in the branches, each living thing relies on this complex balance.

Tim Crosby

Olympic Peninsula

Lena Lake
Quinault Loop Trail
Hoh Hall of Mosses
West Elwha Trail
Upper Dungeness

Nowhere in western Washington will you find the variety of landscapes and climate conditions that exist on the Olympic Peninsula. With its rugged mountains, ocean beaches and dense rain forests, the Olympic Peninsula has areas of heavy rainfall — as much as 12 feet per year on the western side — as well as portions that are semiarid.

Local climates influence which types of trees dominate a forest. Douglas-fir grow mostly in the northern, eastern and southern parts of the peninsula where the climate is drier than the western slopes. This species thrives in sunlight and is the most likely candidate to sprout up after a fire or windstorm. Western hemlock, our state tree, can grow almost anywhere and does well in shade. You'll often find hemlock thriving in the shade of the Douglas-fir, and when a stand of Douglas-fir trees reaches the end of its life cycle, western hemlock emerge as the dominant species, creating what is called a climax forest.

Western redcedar are found in the wetter areas such as the river valleys and lowlands. Sitka spruce predominate on the western side of the Olympics where they thrive in the high rainfall and abundant fog from the ocean.

Lena Lake is in the drier southeastern portion of the Olympics, only about a three-hour drive from Seattle. The valley bottom was logged earlier in the century and much of the rest was decimated by fire, but the stands farther along the Lena Lake Trail are spectacular.

The popular trail starts out wide and easy as it slowly climbs the hillside leading through second-growth trees. It continues to climb gradually as the path narrows and enters magnificent virgin forest. Look for Douglas-fir up to five feet in diameter and western redcedar more than six feet thick. This eastern Olympic forest of Douglas-fir and western hemlock is quite different from the spruce/hemlock forests of the wet west side of the peninsula. In spring, rhododendrons in bloom delight the eye.

After about three miles of steady rise the trail arrives at Lena Lake. The cliffs above look down on the lake surrounded by virgin forest. An excellent campsite in the midst of old growth is at the lake's north end.

The future of these trees is in question. They are temporarily protected under an administrative decision made by the Forest Service. Conservationists hope that eventually Congress will protect the lake and surrounding forest by designating it as wilderness. No trees can be cut in a Congressionally designated wilderness area.

↔ **Getting There:** From Highway 101 turn east onto the Hamma Hamma River Road (Forest Service Road 25) north of Eldon. The Lena Lake trailhead, almost 10 miles after the turnoff, is on the right hand side of the road. No motorized use of the trail is allowed.

Quinault Loop Trail This network of three trails in Lake Quinault's south shore area leads you on educational walks through untouched ancient forests. The trails are well signed, acquainting you with some of their special features. Sitka spruce and western hemlock predominate in this area, but you will also see western redcedar, Douglas-fir and bigleaf maple.

Each trail has its own highlights. Along the Quinault
Loop Trail you encounter a swamp where cedars thrive. Down
the Willaby Creek Trail, an unbelievably huge old cedar stands
proud. The Rain Forest Trail exhibits a classic example of an
ancient forest; some of the Douglas-firs along this trail are up to
eight feet in diameter and nearly 500 years old. All three of
these hikes are easy, but don't hurry — allow a few hours to
truly enjoy all they have to offer.

This is one of the most impressive stands of old-growth
forest in the state. Watch for eagles, blue herons and little
songbirds. Perhaps you'll see an osprey nest. In winter look for
elk. The forest floor is lush, with club mosses, ferns, liverworts
— myriad plants to entrance the botanist or the artist's eye.
Cascara trees, such as those found here, are stripped by local
people who sell bark to laxative manufacturers.

We have Franklin D. Roosevelt to thank for protection of
the Quinault valley. After staying at the Quinault Lodge in
1937, he recommended that much of the north shore of Lake
Quinault be included in Olympic National Park. Unfortu-
nately, the equally majestic south shore was excluded, but part
of the forest has been protected to date by the Forest Service.

↔ *Getting There:* Turn east off Highway 101 onto the
South Shore Road (just south of Amanda Park). Turn right
into the parking lot where the sign says "Quinault Nature
Trail." Signs in the parking lot indicate the lay of the land and
a map of the trails.

Hoh Hall of Mosses If you've never seen a rain forest, take
time to visit the Hoh valley, especially the prime example of
old-growth rain forest called the Hall of Mosses. Club moss,
lichens and licorice fern adorn the trees, adding ever more hues
to the greens of the forest. The Hall of Mosses Trail is very
easy, with only one small hill leading up to the three-quarter-

marbled murrelet

mile loop trail. You will see Sitka spruce — the dominant species in the rainy, cool coastal fog belt from Washington to Alaska — along with western hemlock, Douglas-fir and western redcedar and maple trees. Sitka spruce trunks are straight columns of nearly the same diameter all the way up, with bark in roundish scales. Most dramatic are the old-growth bigleaf maple trees festooned with clinging mosses. The ground is carpeted with emerald leaves looking like huge Irish shamrocks; actually they are oxalis.

Be sure to stop at the visitor information center. Inside you can find out more about the native plants, animals and trees. Other trails that begin and end there give you a chance to explore the different stages of forests as they evolve in the Hoh River valley. In the fall brilliant yellow maple leaves contrast with deep green-needled branches. If you have time, hike for miles up the Hoh trail that eventually climbs to the glaciers of Mount Olympus.

A couple of points of interest on the drive up the Hoh River Road: Don't miss the large Sitka spruce tree on the right side of the road (there is a turnout and a sign). It is reportedly one of the largest in the United States. Notice the dead trees and logs in the Hoh River. These eventually will be washed out to the ocean, then battered back to shore to become some of the driftwood logs you find decorating ocean beaches.

↔ **Getting There:** From Highway 101 turn east on the Hoh River Road (south of Forks and north of Kalaloch). Follow the road 18 miles, past many clearcuts and the entrance to the Olympic National Park to its end in the parking lot.

West Elwha Trail Nestled in the transition zone between the wet and drier sides of the Olympic Peninsula, the Elwha River valley is a mix of virgin forest and second growth. Here, the climate is drier than the coast, but not as dry as the eastern slopes. Douglas-fir, true firs and hemlock thrive here but spruce do not.

Elliott Norse   *Elliott Norse*

The Elwha River, flowing from deep within Olympic
National Park, once was home to a race of 100-pound Chinook
salmon still remembered by oldsters. Salmon migration,
blocked since early in the century by dams, may be restored if
conservationists prevail. Resident fish and the pretty setting
make the river an attraction. Most of us don't think of fish as
part of a forest ecosystem, but they are. The Elwha's giant
salmon attracted hordes of bears and eagles which hauled fish
from the water. Fish scraps were snapped up by the other
foragers and eventually became fish fertilizer enriching the
forest soil.

The West Elwha Trail loosely parallels the Elwha River.
About one mile in, the trail descends to a flat area where a few
old trees remain. The other giants were cut down years ago by
early loggers, before the park was established. The trail continues to the park boundary where the old growth stops.

Look for the horizontal slits — "springboard cuts" — in
the old stumps. In the days before chainsaws, loggers made
these cuts into which they inserted springboards to stand on to
get in better position to saw down the huge trees. Standing
several feet above the ground seems precarious to us, but it was
easier than the alternative: pushing and pulling a crosscut saw
through the flared or swollen base of a tree.

↔ **Getting There:** Turn south onto Elwha Valley Road from Highway 101 (west of Port Angeles). The road follows the Elwha River and, after about 4 miles, enters the Olympic National Park. After the ranger station, turn right onto Boulder Creek Road and cross the river to Altaire Campground. Park in any road turnout nearby if the campground is full. The trailhead is in the campground.

Upper Dungeness Located on the northeastern "rainshadow" side of the Olympics, the Upper Dungeness area gets only 20 inches of rain per year. The trail passes large Douglas-firs in a forest periodically thinned by fire and then rises to dry, higher country that resembles eastern Washington forests, with lodgepole pine and Rocky Mountain juniper.

The first three miles of the Upper Dungeness trail takes you through ancient Douglas-fir forest as it parallels the pristine Dungeness River. At the start of the trail the hill slopes up beside you to allow easy viewing of native plants on a "bench" of nature's garden. The first mile of forest is protected from clearcutting now, but the Forest Service plans to open it up to possible logging.

After one mile on the trail, you arrive at the confluence of Royal Creek and the Dungeness River. Just beyond, the trail enters the Buckhorn Wilderness. From this point on, the old-growth trees are protected by the wilderness designation and will never be logged.

The largest trees continue for another two miles on the trail. Some old trees have charred bark, evidence of past wildfires they have survived. The Upper Dungeness hosts many botanically unusual plants. One of the few areas never covered by ice age glaciers, plants whose closest relatives may be hundreds of miles away were able to survive here.

The trail is easy and fairly level for the first two-and-a-half miles. Beyond, it climbs a hill to reach Camp Handy (a good place to turn around). Backpackers can hike on for miles into Olympic National Park or loop around to the Tubal Cain Trail.

The area is snow-bound in the late fall, winter and early spring because of its higher elevation (2,500 feet) — check with the Quilcene Ranger Station.

↔ *Getting There:* From Highway 101 turn south on Palo Alto Road (1.5 miles west of Sequim Bay State Park). Drive about 8 miles to the junction with Forest Service Road 28. Bear left at the fork onto FS 28. Follow signs from here. Veer right at the sign to East Crossing campground (FS 2860). The road crosses the Dungeness River about 20 miles from Highway 101. A large parking lot is on the right and the trailhead is on the west side of the river near the bridge.

Olympic Peninsula

Don't let these directions scare you — the roads are well marked. You can get a good map that shows Forest Service roads from the ranger station or an outdoor sporting goods store.

Roosevelt elk

Ann Dittmar

Northern Cascades

East Bank

Mountain Loop
Boulder River
White Chuck
North Fork Sauk River
Mount Dickerman
Youth on Age

Skykomish
Troublesome Creek
West Cady Creek
West Cady Ridge

With rugged mountains and many active glaciers, high alpine rivers and lakes, a national park and several wilderness areas, the northern Cascade Mountains supply plenty of recreational opportunities. Ample rainfall makes this area more like the Olympic rain forest than any other mountainous area of Washington state. Many of its ancient forest sites have succumbed to the chain saws, but here are a few samples of stands remaining from the distant past.

East Bank   When Mount Baker was active in the 1840's, embers from the volcano's lava ignited fires which destroyed some of the virgin forest. Mud flows also contributed to the destruction. Trees that survived these and later fires still bear the scars as proof of their battle with the flames. You'll also see charred "chimneys," the outer rims of snags whose rotting cores were burned out. Baker Lake is a popular recreational area offering many scenic views and hikes, a small resort, hot springs, camping, boating and more.

The East Bank Trail (#610), with its fern grotto after fern grotto, follows the Baker Lake shoreline through some of the once-burned area. The hanging growth of vines, moss and ferns, and the new growth everywhere in standing snags and downed logs are excellent examples of the forest life cycle. Woodpecker holes and shelf fungus on a bark-covered trunk help you notice that the tree is dead, but hosts other life.

The four-mile trail is flat and easy, making it ideal for children. They will enjoy the puncheon bridge over a bubbling stream. The trail is good early and late in the year because its low elevation generally keeps it snow free. Yellow violets, trillium or berries can be found in season. Camp or picnic at Anderson Creek or Maple Grove.

This is one trail that can be reached by boat. The Forest Service intends eventually to extend this trail the full length of the eastern side of the lake to connect it with the Baker River Trail. The old Baker River Trail is in the low elevation edge of old-growth forest that extends through privately owned land, up the Baker River and up to Noisy-Diobsud Wilderness and North Cascades National Park.

Though you are unlikely to see them, spotted owls live nearby, and even grizzly bears may wander the farther reaches of the forest. Look for waterfowl on the lake.

This part of the forest will probably not be logged right away, but there is a possibility of timber sales within a few years that could impact the trail.

↔ *Getting There:* From I-5 head east on Highway 20 to the Baker Lake Road (just west of Concrete). Head north on Baker Lake Road, along Grandy Creek and to the Baker Dam/Kulshan Campground Road. Turn right and cross the Upper Baker Dam. Continue .4 of a mile to the "Y" in the road and turn left. The East Bank trailhead is marked by a small sign .7 of a mile further.

Mountain Loop

You may already have traveled the Mountain Loop Highway marveling at the great views and the vivid fall colors, but the old-growth forests easily accessed from the highway offer an excellent reason for a return trip.

The Mountain Loop Highway starts in Darrington on Forest Service Road 20, heads south to Barlow Pass and then east on Highway 92 to Verlot. Paved part way, most of it is a good gravel road. The portion south of Darrington to Silverton is snowbound in winter and the highway often is not plowed. There are too many hikes for one day, so pick a couple and come back to enjoy the others another time. Or stay awhile at a motel or campground.

A stop at the Darrington Ranger Station will give you good information about forests in the area. While at the ranger station, take a minute outside to visit the cross section of a 700-year-old Douglas-fir. In the year 1274 the tree was only four feet tall. By the time the tree died in a slash burn in 1971, it had grown to a whopping nine feet in diameter.

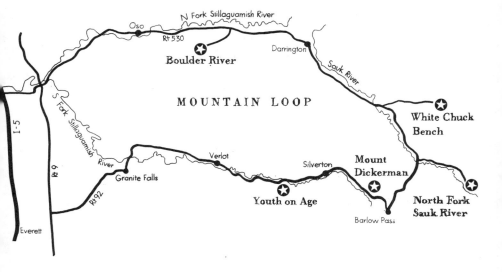

Boulder River The Boulder River Trail, between Arlington and Darrington, west of the mountain loop, is a beautiful walk through a thick, old-growth forest in a lowland river valley. Abundant and exquisite mosses and ferns create a jungle-like atmosphere in some spots. The sights you see along the upper portion of the trail are like what the first settlers in the area found. Now lowland virgin forests are very rare; over the years logging has wiped out almost all low elevation old-growth.

At first, the Boulder River Trail (#734) follows an old railroad logging grade until it reaches the virgin forest with trees up to 750 years old. After about one mile you come to the first of several breathtaking waterfalls. Water crashes down the 200-foot canyon wall into the aptly named Boulder River below. Here the canyon narrows as you enter the dense climax forest. More waterfalls pour down from the walls as you continue up to Boulder Ford Camp, which is a campsite and the trail's end. The well-maintained trail is four miles long.

The best time to see the waterfalls is in the spring and early summer when the snow melt sends more water down the river. The hike is also a good bet in the late fall when higher elevation hikes are covered with snow.

In the river are small rainbow trout. Land animals are more likely to be identified by tracks than actual sightings. Look for signs of cougar, bobcat and black bear. At one time, the steepness of the canyon walls protected the trees from logging, because it was too difficult to build access roads. Since 1984 the area has been protected as a part of the Boulder River Wilderness.

↔ *Getting There:* From I-5 go east on Highway 530 through the town of Oso. Turn south on French Creek Road (Forest Service Road 2010) about 8 miles east of Oso, at mile marker 41. Drive almost 4 miles to where the road switchbacks sharply uphill and park there. The trailhead is at the turn in the road.

northern flying squirrel

White Chuck Bench Trail Giant redcedar trees and river and mountain views highlight this primitive but easily followed trail. The trail, recently restored by The Mountaineers, generally follows the north bank of the White Chuck River. Douglas-fir, western hemlock and western redcedar are seen from the trail. When hiked east to west, the ancient trees are along the first three miles of the seven-mile trail. Another attraction visible from the trail is beaver ponds.

On the drive into the area notice the scarred landscape from clearcutting. These clearcuts are in sharp contrast to the undisturbed area surrounding the trail. More clearcuts may be coming (just south and east of the trailhead is a proposed timber sale area) threatening some of the old trees in the valley.

Conservationists have been trying to protect the White Chuck and surrounding lowland virgin forests since 1927. Their efforts resulted in the creation of the North Cascades National Park and the Glacier Peak Wilderness. But they have not yet succeeded for this valley; most of the White Chuck's forest remains unprotected. The Forest Service proposes to allow the clearcutting of more than half the area upstream from this trail.

↔   *Getting There:* Follow the Mountain Loop Highway (Forest Service Road 20) south from Darrington about 10 miles to the junction of FS 23. Turn east and drive about 6 miles to the bridge that crosses the White Chuck River. Cross the bridge and turn left into the parking area. The sign for the trailhead is on the north side of the parking area near the outhouse.

North Fork Sauk River Trail starts out in a lush rain forest of Douglas-fir with massive old western redcedars up to nine feet in diameter. Feast your eyes on the awesome trees and rich undergrowth.

Giant trees line the first mile of the trail, but the biggest ones are found in the first quarter-mile where the forest is unprotected. After half a mile the trail enters the Glacier Peak Wilderness where, thanks to Congress, the trees are protected from logging. Beyond the first mile the trail passes through a marvelous cedar forest and occasional avalanche swaths. Follow the trail for nearly five miles through grove after grove of cedars, hemlock and Pacific silver fir.

For the more adventuresome: After these five miles, the trail leaves the river and begins to climb. It winds through a series of switchbacks taking you higher and higher to sweeping views, eventually joining the Pacific Crest Trail near the 6,000-foot-high White Pass.

The North Fork Sauk River and Sloan Creek are sandwiched between the Glacier Peak and Henry M. Jackson Wilderness areas. As they did with the White Chuck valley, conservationists urged Congress in vain that much more of this area be protected. The Forest Service has targeted much of the Sloan Creek drainage for clearcutting.

To see this most threatened ancient forest, drive south on Forest Service Road 49 beyond the trailhead for several miles. Some of the trees have already been logged. Elsewhere, blue tags indicate the boundaries of future clearcuts. For splendid views of peaks in the Henry M. Jackson Wilderness, drive on to the end of the road.

↔ **Getting There:** From Darrington drive south on Forest Service Road 20 to the junction with FS 49 (about 17 miles). Take FS 49 east for 7 miles to the North Fork Sauk River Trail (Trail #649). The trailhead is on the east side of the road. There is plenty of parking in the Sloan Creek Campground.

Mount Dickerman This is a steep trail with switchbacks that take you up the side of Mount Dickerman where your efforts are rewarded with spectacular panoramic views. Douglas-firs and western redcedars surround the trail as it ascends the mountain. The trail (#710) is four miles long, but you will find most of the tall older trees in the first mile or so.

You may notice some newer trees growing among the old ones. A fire ran through much of the area in the early 1900's, and it was replanted in 1915.

As you ascend the mountain, take a look at the differences elevation makes in the landscape. The trees become smaller and the vegetation changes. Alaskan yellow cedar, found only at higher elevations, grows high on Mount Dickerman. You will also see spiky subalpine fir. Masses of wild flowers fill the mountain meadows after the snow melts; later in the season wonderful blueberries treat the hiker. This hike is strenuous, with steep switchbacks so allow eight or nine hours for the round trip in addition to driving time. Bring plenty of water.

↔ *Getting There:* Drive south on Forest Service Road 20 about 27 miles from Darrington, and continue past Barlow Pass before heading west on Highway 92. Or drive east from Granite Falls on Highway 92. Watch for the Mount Dickerman trail sign on the north side of the road aproximately 3 miles west of Barlow Pass.

Youth on Age Nature Trail This is a lovely, short walk on an easy, paved trail through old growth. The Douglas-firs along the trail are up to 500 years old, with the biggest just shy of six feet in diameter. Of particular note is an old Pacific silver fir more than five feet in diameter.

This trail is a self-guided nature trail with signs pointing out areas of interest. Be sure to pick up an informative map at the trailhead, the Verlot Public Service Center, or the Darrington Ranger Station.

On the trail are two fine examples of nurse logs. On one, a row of western hemlocks get their start from nutrients of the fallen tree. The other example is quite a bit older — the roots of a large Sitka spruce and those of a western hemlock surround the remains of a nurse log. These examples show how fallen trees provide fertile ground and give life to the next generation.

fisher

The Youth on Age Nature Trail is a flat and easy one-third-mile trail. The trail was paved by the Forest Service to make it accessible for wheelchairs.

This area averages more than 140 inches of rain during the year, so bring your raingear! Due to the high rainfall you'll see Sitka spruce here, an unusual sight in this part of the state. These trees are normally limited to the rainy Olympic Peninsula and wet coastline up to Alaska.

Youth on Age is another name for a plant you may have in your home — *Tolmiea Menziesii* — also known as piggy back. It is the ground cover that abundantly carpets the area; thus the trail name Youth On Age.

↔ **Getting There:** From Darrington go south on Forest Service Road 20 and over Barlow Pass. Head west on Highway 92. Or drive east on Highway 92 from Granite Falls. About 10 miles west of Barlow Pass (8.5 miles east of Verlot Service Center), turn at the Youth on Age sign.

Skykomish

Much of the history of the Skykomish River area, as with all the Northern Cascades, comes from railroad pioneers who opened the way for the flood of settlers. Early parties of railroad surveyors searching for a route to bring the tracks westward ran into trouble in the North Fork Skykomish area. Troublesome Creek gets its name from the difficulties they had in establishing a suitable railroad grade east of this torrential stream.

West Cady Creek and West Cady Ridge Trail bear the name of the chief surveyor who had mapped a route along the North Fork of the Skykomish River. Ironically, Cady's route was never used. The rails were laid along the South Fork and went over Stevens Pass by way of a tunnel.

Troublesome Creek The tumbling Troublesome Creek cuts through a textbook old-growth grove. A half-mile, well-main-

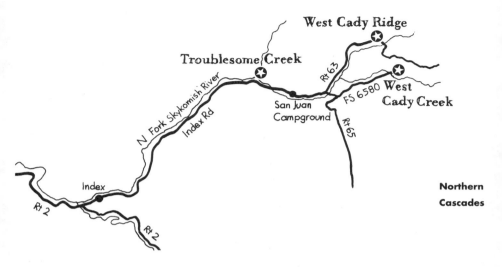

tained trail begins and ends in the Troublesome Creek Campground and follows both sides of the creek. Along the trail
you'll find a mix of young, intermediate and old-growth trees.
Miners who worked gold, silver and copper claims as far as two
miles upstream were the original users of the Troublesome
Creek Trail. The trail ends at the upper bridge, but a faint old
miners' trail continues north for another mile and a half on the
west side.

High winds have felled many trees on the western edge of
the grove. Some of the windfalls are close to the trail and allow
you to inspect their root systems. Roots of the Northwest's
giant conifers are frequently shallow. They function well in
gathering nutrients from the rich upper soil layer, but as you can
see, they may not protect the trees from blowing over in the
high winds of a winter storm.

Notice the unusual deep blue-green color of the creek.
The color comes from the minerals in the rocks that have dis-
solved in the water.

↔ **Getting There:** Turn off Highway 2 (Stevens Pass Highway) onto the Index Road and head 11.5 miles northeast to the Troublesome Creek Campground. At this writing there were no signs on the road after it leaves Highway 2, but the Forest Service designates it as FS 63. Start your hike from either side of the creek.

West Cady Creek The big trees on West Cady Creek stand in an unprotected but wild area untouched by roads, improved trails or other signs of humans. This extensive stand of old forest provides an opportunity to wander alone through an undisturbed ancient forest along a roaring creek. Many old growth connoisseurs consider the West Cady Creek area a superior example of an ancient forest.

Huge Douglas-firs up to five feet in diameter and more than 200 feet tall line the undeveloped trail, along with western redcedar, western hemlock and Pacific silver fir.

↔ **Getting There:** From Highway 2 turn onto Index Road. Keep driving past the Troublesome Creek campground (notice the old growth on either side of the road as you pass the campground) and San Juan campground. At 14.5 miles from Highway 2 the paved portion of the road ends. You will reach a junction .7 mile farther. Take the right fork, following Forest Service Road 65 (as of this writing it is still signed with its old number, FS 280). Turn left onto FS 6580. The road climbs through clearcuts, and at 3 miles you see a giant Douglas-fir, well over six feet in diameter. This behemoth marks the start of a strip of old growth along West Cady Creek. Drive .5 mile past the big Douglas-fir to the road's end.

Park at the end of the road, cross over the small brook and go about 300 feet to where the trail drops down to the right toward the creek. Follow the bulldozer trail along the lower edge of the clearcut almost to the end of the clearcut to a slash pile. Follow the faint trail into the cathedral-like forest. The trail may be difficult to follow from this point on, but the open terrain and the roaring creek make direction finding possible. A map would be helpful.

West Cady Ridge The West Cady Ridge Trail (#1054) takes you vertically through an upper elevation stand of ancient trees outside of the Henry M. Jackson Wilderness. As you climb up the ridge, the species and mix of trees change with the elevation.

Cross the thundering gorge of North Fork Skykomish River on the footbridge and, after nearly a mile, start climbing switchbacks. The Sierra Club and a horse riding group have "adopted" this trail and the first two miles are in good condition. Beyond that the way may be badly rutted. At lower elevations, dens of devil's club and shoals of skunk cabbage line the hollows of minor drainages along with huckleberry, ferns, moss and lichens. Elk tracks may be visible in wet spots on the trail.

On your way up the ridge, the trees become smaller and silver fir more dominant. Here and there, pockets of Douglas-fir and cedar giants grow in fertile patches of soil. After three steep miles, the trail reaches the ridge and follows it five more miles up through alpine vegetation to the Pacific Crest Trail. Along the way you enter the Henry M. Jackson Wilderness and are treated to spectacular views from Benchmark Mountain.

↔ ***Getting There:*** Turn off Highway 2 onto Index Road as it follows the North Fork of the Skykomish River. Go past Troublesome Creek and San Juan campgrounds to the junction of Forest Service Roads now numbered 63 and 65 (as of this writing they were still signed 280 and 290, respectively). Turn left on FS 63, drive 4.5 miles and cross the Quartz Creek bridge. After 200 feet you will find the trailhead on the south side of the road opposite the Quartz Creek trailhead.

fringed myotis

Tim Crosby

Central Cascades

Federation Forest State Park
The Dalles Campground
Camp Sheppard
Snoquera Falls
Skookum Flats
Grove of the Patriarchs

Highway 410 along the White River is an often-travelled road, leading many Puget Sounders to Mount Rainier in search of scenery and recreation. Along the way are several sites within easy reach of the highway which contain some of the few remaining old-growth stands at lower elevations.

Ancient Douglas-fir, western redcedar and western hemlock trees are the most typical old-growth species at low elevation of the Cascades. In autumn, alder and vine maple brilliantly color the hillsides.

Elk, deer and bear frequent the area as they forage for food and drink from the White River.

Federation Forest State Park Federation Forest State Park offers a perfect introduction to old growth and maintains a very informative Interpretive Center, open Wednesday through Sunday in season. A network of well-marked trails includes two short loops. One is a little less than a mile long, the other about a half-mile. Signs along the trails identify the many sights, and you can borrow a guidebook from the interpretive center for more detailed explanations.

If you have to choose between the loops, pick the longer one to the west. The West Trail meanders through what is called "Land of the Giants" where you will come across some enormous old Douglas-fir and some of the largest western red-cedar in the state.

Part of this trail connects with the historic Naches trail, which ran between Walla Walla and Fort Steilacoom. Pioneers migrating west used this trail until 1884 when an easier route was cut through a lower pass in the Cascades. With the exception of the nearby highway and its occasional traffic noises, this forest is just what the pioneers encountered as they traveled toward Puget Sound.

Through the efforts of a group of tenacious women, this state park is here today. The Washington State Federation of Women's Clubs in cooperation with the state legislature opened Big Trees State Park west of Snoqualmie Pass in 1928. Wind, fire and the axe were the demise of that park in the 1930's, but a new park — Federation Forest State Park — was opened on this site in its stead.

↔ **Getting There:** Heading east on Highway 410, turn right at the Interpretive Center sign approximately 17 miles east of Enumclaw and park in the center's lot. The trails begin next to the center. Federation Forest is officially open from April 15 to October 31, but individuals can use the trails any time of year.

The Dalles Campground Nestled among 300-year-old towering Douglas-fir trees is The Dalles Campground, a pretty spot where each campsite is sheltered by the sweeping branches of these giants. The campground's center attraction is an impressive 700-year-old Douglas-fir, so mammoth that were it cut down, it would provide enough lumber for eight homes.

This tree is a survivor. It survived a fire that swept through the area more than 300 years ago, killing all other trees. If you inspect the bark you will see the black scars that flames left behind. The tree was probably able to live through the inferno because of its age at the time. Older Douglas-fir trees have thick bark that insulates them against the intense heat of a forest fire.

coast mole

↔ **Getting There:** Turn right off Highway 410 at The Dalles campground sign, approximately 26 miles east of Enumclaw. There is limited parking available for those who just want to see the oldest tree. The Dalles campground is open from Memorial Day weekend to Labor Day weekend.

Camp Sheppard Camp Sheppard, a Boy Scout Camp 28 miles east of Enumclaw, is the point from which two trails escort you through ancient forests and offer views of dramatic waterfalls. The Boy Scout Camp area is open to all visitors, even when the camp is in session. The land is managed by the U. S. Forest Service which means that it is yours to use, too.

Snoquera Falls The Snoquera Falls Trail starts in Camp Sheppard. The trail originates in the parking lot and is marked by two parallel logs. Just past the trailhead you enter a Douglas-fir grove. Take a left turn at the trail junction and hike up the hill to the base of Snoquera Falls. As it climbs the hillside above Camp Sheppard, the Snoquera Falls Trail leads you through old-growth Douglas-fir trees, where moss blankets the ground.

This one-and-three-quarter-mile trail takes you from 2,400 to about 3,100 feet in elevation. There are a few switchbacks along the way, making this a moderately strenuous hike.

The falls that await you at the high point in the trail are a spectacular sight in the spring, but the view is definitely well worth the hike any other time of the year. If you turn to look out over the White River Valley, you will enjoy another wonderful scenic vista.

↔ **Getting There:** Heading southeast on Highway 410 turn left into Camp Sheppard. The camp is approximately 28 miles east of Enumclaw. There is plenty of parking available.

Camp Sheppard is open year-round, but at times during the winter snow may prohibit hiking. Make sure to check the snow levels before a wintertime visit to this site.

Skookum Flats The Skookum Flats Trail is fairly flat and easy, leading you through beautiful old-growth Douglas-fir and western redcedar trees. Hike along the river bank next to the lava cliff for about two and a quarter miles. There you are treated to Skookum Falls and Skookum Seeps, where water seeps out of the moss covered basalt cliff above you.

Skookum Flats is across the highway from Camp Sheppard. The best place to park is in the Camp Sheppard lot. Then, walk south along Highway 410 to approximately 100 yards past milepost 53. A small sign (six feet down the bank from the road) marks the start of the trail that will take you to the Skookum Flats Trail. As a special treat along the way you'll cross the White River via a fun, cable-suspension bridge that was built by the Boy Scouts. Once over the bridge, follow the trail downstream.

↔ *Getting There:* See the directions for Camp Sheppard. The Skookum Flats Trail is difficult, if not impossible, in the snow without the help of cross-country skis or snowshoes. Be sure to check the snow level before planning a trip during the winter. The elevation of the trail is 2,400 feet.

Grove of the Patriarchs is a magnificent, virgin grove of western redcedar, western hemlock and Douglas-fir on an island in the middle of the Ohanapecosh River in Mount Rainier National Park. If you are starting your journey from Seattle, it is quite a drive — about three hours each way.

The trees along this trail are huge and estimated to be almost 1,000 years old. They have survived all these years largely because they are protected from fire by the river that surrounds the island.

The trail starts behind the restrooms at the parking lot and leads you about a half-mile to a junction. Turn right at the junction and cross the suspension bridge spanning the Ohanapecosh River. Once on the island, the trail continues briefly

Tim Crosby

before it forks. It is a loop, one-and-a-half miles in length, so
you can go either way.

↔   ***Getting There:*** Take Highway 410 south toward Mount
Rainier to the junction of Highway 123. Take Highway 123
south, from Cayuse Pass. Turn right onto the Stevens Canyon
Road past the park entrance. There is a parking lot about a
quarter-mile from the highway and the trailhead is behind the
restrooms. Grove of the Patriarchs is open from mid-May to
November.

deer mouse

Bob Pearson

Southern Cascades

Big Hollow
Cedar Flats
Lewis River
Quartz Creek
Upper Clear Creek
Green River
Upper Yellowjacket

The Gifford Pinchot National Forest is a vast and varied forest land. It covers 1.3 million acres stretching from Mount Rainier to the Columbia River and from Mount St. Helens to Mount Adams. The biggest tourist attraction in this area is Mount St. Helens; many visitors come to the southern part of the state to see the devastation from the volcano's 1980 eruption.

What these visitors may miss are the significant stands of old growth located in some lesser known parts of Mount St. Helens National Volcanic Monument and the Gifford Pinchot National Forest.

The largest unprotected roadless area in western Washington (outside of a designated wilderness area) is the Dark Divide. Three of the trips (Quartz Creek, Upper Clear Creek and Upper Yellowjacket) described in this section are forests in or adjacent to the Dark Divide Roadless Area.

Big Hollow The largest unfragmented ancient forest between Lewis River and the Columbia River is Big Hollow in the Bourbon Roadless Area, located just east of Trapper Creek Wilderness. Douglas-fir, western hemlock, western redcedar, Pacific silver fir, noble fir and western white pine are found in various parts of the Bourbon Roadless Area. Northern spotted owls live here. Lower reaches of three creeks host steelhead trout that

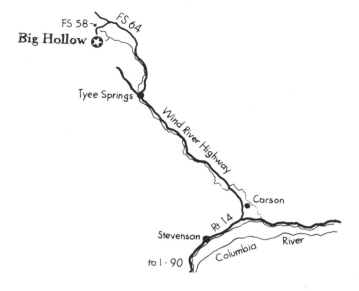

migrate up Wind River from the Columbia. Big Hollow Trail is one of several trails in this rugged land.

Big Hollow Trail (#158) may be disrupted by clearcuts at its eastern trailhead. Leave a car here, if you can, but start your hike from the other end. Take Observation Trail (#132) south through old-growth silver fir in Sisters Rocks Research Natural Area. At the Research Natural Area boundary you reach open meadows and berry fields where a fire cleared the forest in 1902. Western white pine adorn the slopes. Soon you reach the junction with Big Hollow Trail and a campsite under the trees.

Hike down through natural second-growth forest regrowing after the burn. It inherited the legacy of earlier old growth — the many huge snags and downed logs provide wildlife habitat. As you descend, you'll find more and more large live trees until you are fully in old growth. The steepness of the hillside allows you to see into the canopy of ancient branches. After about two miles in ancient Douglas-fir forest, you reach Big Hollow Creek. Ford the creek. You'll get your feet wet, but it is not far to the road.

pine marten

The Forest Service anticipates selling timber in a considerable part of the Bourbon Roadless Area in 1991.

↔   *Getting There:* Take I-5 to I-205 to Highway 14, which you follow through Camas and Stevenson. Turn north on Wind River Highway (which becomes Forest Service Road 30) and go approximately 13 miles toward Government Mineral Springs. At Tyee Springs turn right on FS 64. In about 4 miles at a hairpin turn, the eastern trailhead for Big Hollow Trail should still be visible. Continue on FS 64 to FS 58 to Sisters Rocks Research Natural Area and the north end of Observation Trail. Park by the roadside. Walk through the Research Natural Area to the junction with Big Hollow Trail and down the trail to FS 64. A map would be helpful.

Cedar Flats Discover the serenity of this ancient forest of western redcedar and Douglas-fir on an easy family hike. Cedar Flats Nature Trail is a one-mile loop through a Research Natural Area, set aside to protect an area of old growth for study. Here scientists investigate many aspects of nature to gain insights into the wonders of this complex ecosystem.

The stand is dominated by western redcedar nearly 200 feet tall. The dense, multi-layered canopy screens out most of the light on the forest floor. The shade has thinned out the smaller trees and undergrowth making it easy to see mosses, ferns and other old-growth vegetation of the forest floor.

As you start your walk, look to the north to see an unfamiliar sight — a giant cedar snag whose broken crown provides fertile soil from which seedlings sprouted. Along the way you'll see more common examples of nurse logs on the ground passing their nutrients onto the next generation. Fallen trees lie at odd angles on the forest floor. When these trees fell, they ricocheted off neighboring trees.

Listen and watch for elk in the forest and down along the banks of the Muddy River.

↔ **Getting There:** Take I-5 to Woodland (exit 21) and go east 29 miles on Highway 503 to Cougar. Beyond Cougar the road becomes Forest Service Road 90. Continue east toward the Pine Creek Information Center at the east end of Swift Reservoir. Go straight on FS 25 for about 3.7 miles to the Cedar Flats Trail entrance on the right side of the road.

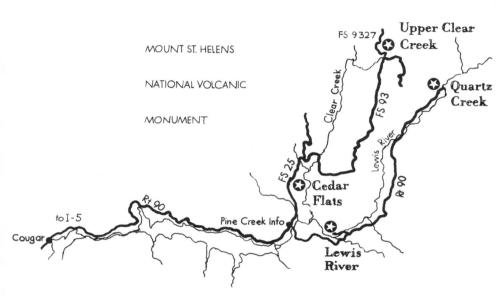

Lewis River A spectacular view of the Curly Creek waterfall as it spills into the Lewis River is at the beginning of a trail through a large ancient forest. Lewis River Trail (#31) plunges into a forest of aged Douglas-fir, western redcedar and western hemlock. Some of the trees in this river valley are more than 500 years old; they would have been seedlings about the time Columbus sailed for the New World.

A fairly level trail as far as Bolt Shelter (about two and a half miles) makes this an easy hike for all ages. Because of its low elevation, it is generally snow free all year. Beyond Bolt Shelter the trail climbs up and down over rocky bluffs. The trail is nine and a half miles long, usually within sight or sound of the river. You'll walk in old growth for about the first four miles of the trail. Beyond the point where Big Creek enters the Lewis River (on the opposite bank) the trail goes through natural forest that has regrown after a forest fire of about 1920. Take in at least the first three miles to experience some great examples of ancient trees. To hike the entire trail, leave one car at the west (downstream) trailhead and drive to the east (upstream) trailhead. The hike is best when heading downstream.

↔ *Getting There:* Take I-5 to Woodland (exit 21) and go east 29 miles on Highway 503 to Cougar. Highway 503 becomes Forest Service Road 90, which goes east to the Pine Creek Information Center. Go right on FS 90 at the junction of FS 90 and FS 25. FS 90 takes you through the hamlet of Eagles Cliff and along the Lewis River. At 5.2 miles turn left (northwest) on FS 9039 which takes you across the river. The trail starts by the bridge, but be sure to drive .25 mile farther to the Forest Service parking lot to see Curly Creek Falls.

Quartz Creek Many creeks, lakes and ridges in Washington bear the name "Quartz." There are two Quartz Creeks in old-growth stands in the Gifford Pinchot National Forest. The Quartz Creek described here is part of the Dark Divide Roadless Area. The other, near the north end of Mount St. Helens National Volcanic Monument, is listed in "More Ancient Forest Areas" in the back of this guidebook.

Quartz Creek is a beautiful setting in an increasingly rare resource — low elevation virgin forest. Many trees are three to four feet in diameter; some are bigger. The trail goes through two clearcuts already and this area is a prime candidate for future logging because its many large trees are easily accessible. The Forest Service has no current plans to sell this timber, but plans could change and trees could be sold at any time.

Quartz Creek Trail (#5) isn't easy. Platinum Creek is challenging to cross, and the trail goes up and down along the way although the net elevation gain is only a few hundred feet. For the best views of old growth, follow the trail up to the Snagtooth Creek crossing (about four and a half miles), then head back. The best old growth starts just after the second clearcut (about two and a half miles).

Look for evidence of deer, elk and coyote on the trail, and if you're unusually lucky you may see a flying squirrel.

↔ **Getting There:** See the directions to Lewis River. Stay on Forest Service Road 90. The trailhead is about 17.5 miles from the junction of FS 90 and FS 25 and is just before the Quartz Creek bridge.

Upper Clear Creek Wright Meadow Trail (#80) takes you into Washington's longest continuous corridor of old-growth Douglas-fir outside of Olympic National Park, a forest corridor more than ten miles long.

Follow the trail about a mile and a half to Clear Creek. Here Elk Creek joins Clear Creek from the northwest in a magnificent canyon. A spectacular waterfall is just downstream on Clear Creek. To continue on the trail you must ford the creek, a difficult task unless the water is low. The trail now ends in a clearcut but may be rebuilt to connect with Forest Service Road 25. Check with the Mount St. Helens Ranger District to find out about the status of the extension. This is a somewhat strenuous hike that drops 1,300 feet to the creek, then climbs 800 feet travelling from east to west.

For those experienced in off-trail hiking, Clear Creek offers one of the last opportunities to explore a forest relatively unimpaired by roads or logging. Use a map and compass to

Vaux's swift

navigate. Look for impressive views of waterfalls and Clear Creek Canyon. Marvel at western redcedar and Douglas-fir averaging six feet in diameter.

Trout fishing in Clear Creek is superb thanks to the old-growth habitat. Log jams from the fallen giants and the woody debris make ideal locations for fish to feed and spawn.

↔ *Getting There:* See directions to Cedar Flats. Continue 1 mile, crossing the Muddy River. Forest Service Road 25 begins to climb steeply. At a sharp left curve, look for the junction with FS 93, and take that road. FS 93 takes you east and then north about 15 miles to FS 9327. Go to the left on FS 9327 and head north past Wright Meadow. At about 1.5 miles, look for the trailhead.

Green River (in Mount St Helens National Monument)

Shielded from Mount St. Helens by high ridges, about two-thirds of the old growth Douglas-fir in the Green River "Valley of the Giants" survived the 1980 eruption. The Forest Service reopened the reconstructed Green River Trail (#213) in summer of 1989. It is a five-mile (one way) hike in a deep valley forest of trees more than 400 years old. As part of Mount St. Helens National Volcanic Monument this forest is permanently protected from logging.

Mines and miners' cabins dating back more than 60 years are along the trail. The Minnie Lee cabin is an impressive structure built of massive logs, now gradually being recycled back into the forest. Watch for herds of elk in the valley, especially in the fall.

↔ *Getting There:* Take Highway 12 to Randle; turn south on Cispus Road. Go 1 mile to a "Y" and take the right fork (straight ahead) which becomes Forest Service Road 25. About 10 miles from Randle take FS 26 as it forks right off FS 25. Go 12 miles and turn right on FS 2612 which you follow to the trailhead.

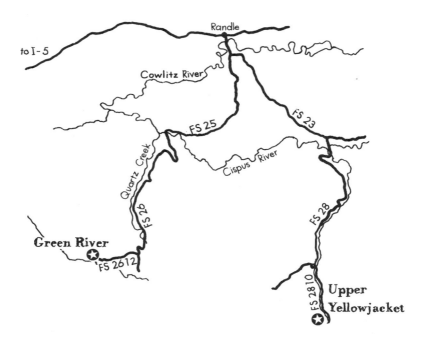

Upper Yellow Jacket A world-record noble fir stands proudly in a group of four noble firs in the vicinity of clearcuts. Noble firs are the biggest of the true fir species, and this is the largest known noble fir anywhere. It is more than 200 feet tall with a diameter more than six feet. Although this current record-holder may lose some of its height because the top portion is dying, several candidates nearby are ready to take its place.

It is unusual to see such a concentration of oversized trees of this species. Moist rich soil at higher elevation combined with abundant sunlight created ideal growing conditions to produce the world-record and other large noble firs. Douglas-fir does not do as well in this moderately high elevation and gives way to the better suited noble fir. You can tell an old noble fir by its ashy brown bark divided by deep fissures into rectangular plates, and by its stiff, closely spaced needles that make each twig look like a brush.

There is no formal trail here (a map would be helpful), but you can wander around the area surrounding the enormous tree and admire the other very old trees. Explore the Forest Service roads to the south. About half a mile south of the largest fir the main road makes a sharp left, but an unmarked dirt road (Forest Service Road 051) continues south. Walk up this winding, unmaintained road. In about a mile, after crossing three forks of Yellowjacket Creek, you enter still another stand of enormous noble firs. This exploration can be a good one-day outing, or it can be part of an extended trip on the Boundary Trail (#1). The Forest Service plans timber sales in this area.

↔ *Getting There:* Take Highway 12 east from I-5 to Randle. For road and trail information stop at the Randle Ranger Station on the east end of town. From Randle, take Cispus Road (FS Roads 23 and 25) 1 mile to the "Y" in the road. Take the left fork (east), follow FS 23 for 9 miles and then turn right on FS 28. The pavement ends beyond the bridge over Yellowjacket Creek, but stay on FS 28. After following Yellowjacket Creek for about 2 miles, watch for a towering seven-foot-diameter Douglas-fir as you pass below Langille Peak on the left. You are likely to see deer here.

After 10 miles continue south on FS 2810 rather than the main fork to the right. Drive 3.5 miles to a grassy, flat area with young alder trees. Across the stream, several hundred yards away and surrounded by a fence, stands the record-holding noble fir.

Townsend chipmunk

Tim Crosby

Puget Sound Area

Schmitz Park
Seward Park
Asahel Curtis Nature Trail
Point Defiance Park
South Whidbey State Park
Deception Pass State Park

Old trees still stand near urban areas. Through the protection of city and state parks, some of these ancient trees have been able to survive the growth of the cities; they serve as a reminder of what the Puget Sound area was like before settlers came and the forest changed its face.

The old trees you'll find in the parks are not, by definition, old-growth forest. In most cases there are too few trees, not enough wildlife and a lack of the biological diversity you would find in a wild forest. These groves are all that's left of the old growth that once blanketed the area. But the trees are still big, very old and impressive. Consider these places an introduction to other more complete forests.

The sites in this section are close enough to the Everett-Seattle-Tacoma area for an afternoon getaway or a picnic. Discover the ancient wonders practically in the cities' back yard.

Schmitz Park Who would believe there is an eight-foot-diameter Douglas-fir still standing in West Seattle? There is, and it is a highlight of Schmitz Park. A half-mile loop trail escorts you through the grove of huge Douglas-firs and western redcedar and past a lovely gurgling stream fed by two tributaries. In this microcosm of forest, all the characteristics that define old-growth forest can be seen: large trees and small of numerous

pileated woodpecker

species, large standing snags, big logs on the ground and in the stream. In the core of the park the undergrowth is as luxuriant and diverse as a deep forest.

Most of the land that is now Schmitz Park was donated to the city in 1908. The donors were Park Commissioner Ferdinand Schmitz and his wife Emma. The couple wished to preserve some of the original forest that greeted the first settlers.

↔ **Getting There:** Head west on the West Seattle Bridge; exit onto Admiral Way. Stay on Admiral Way, go through the business district and downhill toward the sound. The entrance is on the left just before the bridge over a ravine.

Seward Park Take a walk through a forest in the city. This trail through the giants takes you back in time, back to what Seattle was like before skyscrapers and hydroplanes. From the sights and sounds of the trail, you'd never know you were in the city (unless it's a busy summer weekend!). Even when Seward Park is crowded, few people walk on the trails through its woods.

Seward Park has been in the hands of the city for almost 100 years. Before the Lake Washington ship canal was built, Seward Park was an island. When the water level in Lake Washington was lowered, the connecting land was uncovered making the island into a peninsula.

One of the tallest trees holds an eagle's nest; it can be seen from a parking lot off Lake Washington Boulevard but not from the ground below. Douglas-fir, western redcedar and knobby old maples are survivors of the original forest, as are ferns, salal and Oregon grape. Try to ignore the weeds, but watch out for poison oak.

↔ **Getting There:** Going south on Lake Washington Boulevard, south of I-90, turn left at the entrance to Seward Park. Park in the lot that is almost at the crest of the hill. The trailhead is across the road. You can take Metro bus #39 to Seward Park; call Metro for details.

 vagrant shrew

Asahel Curtis Nature Trail Unless you noticed the ragged and unsymmetrical tops of the old-growth trees from I-90, you'd never know an old-growth forest existed right off the freeway. It has Douglas-fir, western hemlock, western redcedar, western white pine, Pacific silver fir and noble fir — one of the last old-growth stands in the I-90 corridor. Some of these trees got their start in the thirteenth century and are more than 250 feet high; one is more than 19 feet in girth.

Puget
Sound
Area

A relatively flat, self-guided trail about a mile long leads you through the forest. Look for signs identifying various species of trees. Notice, as you walk, the dead snags and downed logs; these are necessary for the health of an old-growth forest. The decaying matter provides food, shelter and nutrients for its inhabitants. The stand is fairly small, but if you could block out the freeway noise you might imagine yourself here decades ago with the naturalist and photographer for whom it is named, Asahel Curtis.

↔ *Getting There:* Heading west on I-90 from Seattle take exit 47 (Denny Creek/Asahel Curtis) and after exiting turn right; do not cross the freeway. Follow the signs for Asahel Curtis. At Forest Service Road 55, turn left and drive .5 mile to the end of the road and the parking lot for the trail.

Point Defiance Park Point Defiance Park is well known for its beautiful views, numerous activities and beautifully maintained floral gardens. There is something for everyone here: a zoo, an aquarium, Fort Nisqually, a boathouse, beaches, trails and roads winding through the whole park. There is even an replica of an old logging camp at Camp Six. Tacoma residents are justifiably proud of these special grounds.

What is not well-known, however, is that there are Douglas-firs more than seven feet in diameter here. One tree, the Mountaineer Tree, started growing about the time Shakespeare was born, in 1564. This giant is more than 200 feet tall.

The park is big — 700 acres — and ranks as the twelfth largest city park in the United States. The peninsula was used by the Hudson's Bay Company as a fur trading post in the mid 1800's. It was then used as a military reservation until the city of Tacoma obtained the land in 1905.

↔ *Getting There:* From I-5 take exit 132 (southwest of the Tacoma Dome) to Highway 16. Heading northeast take the 6th Avenue exit and turn left. Within one block turn right onto Pearl Street and drive directly into the park. Once in the park, follow the signs for Five Mile Drive. Many trails lead off Five Mile Drive; the old growth is throughout the northern end of the peninsula.

South Whidbey Island State Park Three trails here show you a rare sight: a virgin forest bordering Puget Sound. The Forest Discovery Trail is a loop from the first parking lot to the second. Pick up a sketch map at either trailhead or at the ranger's office. This trail offers great views of the sound to the west and of mighty Douglas-fir, grand fir, western redcedar, and western hemlock in the forest. Variety is the highlight of this walk. You'll see everything from a cedar swamp to licorice fern to Sitka spruce trees.

The Beach Trail descends to the beach from the main parking lot, leading you through salmonberry, elderberry, blackberry, bigleaf maple trees and alder as well as large conifers. The Hobbit Trail, starting near campsite 23, is equally interesting. Both the Hobbit and Beach trails have steep steps down the bluff. Walking along the beach allows you to make a loop trip of these two trails.

Another trail, The Wilbert Trail, starts across the road from the park entrance and goes into the Classic U Forest. The trail is named for Harry Wilbert, one of the leaders of the citizens' group who built the trail. It's another easy walk through very old Douglas-fir and western redcedar.

The citizens of Whidbey Island came to the rescue of a portion of this forest in 1978 when it was threatened with clearcutting. The state Department of Natural Resources planned to cut the timber for revenue. Whidbey Island residents took the department to court and won. Now the State Parks Commission is buying the land to protect the old growth and add it to the park.

↔ *Getting There:* Going north on Highway 525 from the ferry terminal at Clinton on Whidbey Island, turn left on Bush Point Road (north of Freeland). Bush Point Road becomes Smugglers Cove Road and takes you to the entrance of South Whidbey Island State Park on the left. Drive past the ranger station and turn right and then left into the paved parking lot. A seven-foot-diameter Douglas-fir with burn scars on its bark greets you in the parking lot.

Deception Pass State Park The Hoypus Point Trail on Coronet Bay is an easy walk through a small stand of western hemlock, western redcedar and very large Douglas-fir. Several side trails invite exploration. Beautiful views of Mount Baker and the Cascades appear as you leave the old-growth. Be on the lookout for bald eagles, woodpeckers and deer.

Look closely at the undergrowth in the forest — notice the mosses, ferns, salal, Oregon grape and salmonberry, and the mushrooms that appear unexpectedly. A rich diversity of plant life awaits you in other areas of the park as well, from cranberries and labrador tea to dune grass and sand verbena.

The park has a plethora of recreational opportunities: fishing, boating, swimming, hiking, bicycling, scuba diving, bird-watching and picnicking. More than 18 miles of trails run throughout the park. And there are plenty of campsites.

Deception Pass gets its name from Captain George Vancouver's confusion. Vancouver first named what he thought was an inlet, Port Gardner. When he discovered that the inlet

northern spotted owl

was really a narrow passage between two islands, he renamed it Deception Pass.

↔   *Getting There:* From Anacortes, head south on Highway 20 for about 9 miles and cross the high bridge over Deception Pass. Turn east onto Coronet Bay Road (south of the south entrance to Deception Pass State Park). Continue on Coronet Bay Road for about 1 mile past the marina and picnic area to a turnout on the right side of the road. The trail begins at the white gate beside the long wooden fence. This site is about a two-and-a-half-hour drive from Seattle.

David Dittmar

The Future of Ancient Forests

Walking through an ancient forest is a humbling experience. There among the majestic giants is a way of life, an ecosystem that has evolved and thrived for a hundred centuries.

Today all we have left is a fragmented sample of the magnificent forest that once carpeted the Northwest. From these few fragments we gather not only the knowledge of our history, but keys to our future — new foods and medicines, clean air and water.

Seemingly strong and timeless, yet so threatened, the few remaining stands of old-growth forests are at our mercy. What a shame it would be to have only pictures someday.

The future of most of the remaining old-growth stands lies in the decisions being made by the U.S. Forest Service and elected officials. If you are concerned about the future of your favorite segment of ancient forest, or about old growth in general, take its future into your own hands.

Ways to Help:

Introduce the ancient trees to your friends nationwide so that more people will appreciate their special place in our heritage.

Join one or more of the organizations working to save the Northwest's ancient forests, such as The Wilderness Society.

Write to the Forest Service to let them know your opinion of the value of old-growth forests and, in particular, describe the stands you know and love.

When you visit the old trees, stop in at the Ranger District office and let the staff know your concerns.

Tell your Senators and Representative what you think about ancient forests. Ask that decisions about federal forest management policies reflect the importance of protecting our groves of old trees. Local leaders need to hear from you too.

Write letters to the editors of your local newspapers and to the editorial boards of your TV and radio stations.

Most important, as you grow weary of bureaucratic maneuvering necessary to protect our forests, take a break. Go back to the woods. Listen to the silence. Breathe deep of the scented air. Stretch your legs where the ground is covered with needles. Stretch your neck to see the tops of giant trees. Look, listen, smell, feel — and experience renewal from the ancient places.

Wherever your home is, you can write to the President and to your own Senators and Representative. The national forests belong to all Americans.

President George Bush
The White House
Washington, DC 20500

Senator _____
U.S. Senate
Washington, DC 20510

Honorable _____
U.S. House of Representatives
Washington, DC 20515

If you live in Washington state, your senators (as of 1989) are Senator Brock Adams and Senator Slade Gorton. Your representative is one of the following: John Miller, 1st District; Al Swift, 2nd District; Jolene Unsoeld, 3rd District; Sid Morrison, 4th District; Tom Foley, 5th District; Norm Dicks, 6th District; Jim McDermott, 7th District; Rod Chandler, 8th District. *You can telephone the Capitol switchboard at 202-224-3121.*

Washington state officials:

Governor Booth Gardner
Washington State Legislative Bldg.
Olympia, WA 98504

Brian Boyle,
Commissioner of Public Lands
Dept. of Natural Resources
Olympia, WA 98504

Forest Service officials:

Chief of U.S. Forest Service
P.O. Box 96090
Washington, DC 20090

Regional Forester
319 S.W. Pine St.
Portland, OR 97208

For the addresses of the forest supervisors and district rangers, see page 72. For addresses of your local press and broadcast stations, please refer to your telephone book.

More Ancient Forest Areas

Ancient forests can be visited in a number of other places, some of which are listed below. Numerous excellent hiking books (see Bibliography) and maps are available at book and outdoor equipment stores.

Abbreviations used in the following:

FS   = Forest Service
FS-ROG   = Forest Service Recreational Opportunity Guide
             (ROGs can be obtained at most Forest Service
             Ranger Districts.)
TRIS   = Trail Information System
             *This computerized data base has current trail inform-
             ation and conditions available at the Seattle office of
             the Forest Service, the public libraries in downtown
             Seattle, Olympia, Ellensburg and Yakima, and
             Recreational Equipment Inc. in Seattle and Bellevue.*

Olympic Peninsula

Gray Wolf River A small spectacular stand in a fire scarred mosaic. Located in the northeast portion of the Olympic National Forest and Park near Sequim, partly protected in the Buckhorn Wilderness. *Olympic Mountains Trail Guide*, pages 96-97.

Lower Big Quilcene River Trail In an area of many clearcuts and second growth, there are gorgeous ancient trees between the trail and the river before the first river crossing. *Olympic Mountains Trail Guide*, page 123.

Duckabush River A strenuous hike. The old growth is before the Big Hump area. *Olympic Mountains Trail Guide*, page 151.

Upper South Fork Skokomish A splendid example of an ancient forest. Large old Douglas-fir, silver fir, western hemlock and redcedar along the river in the southeast portion of the Olympics. Access road is closed until April 30. *Olympic Mountains Trail Guide*, page 203.

More
Areas

Maple Glade Nature Trail New trail (1988) on the north side of Lake Quinault. Visit the Quinault Ranger Station for information.

Queets Rain Forest Must ford a dangerous, fast flowing river to get to the trailhead and to the miles of rain forest. *Olympic Mountains Trail Guide*, page 247.

Rugged Ridge Trail High elevation hemlock and silver fir on a short steep trail adjacent to the Olympic National Park boundary. Much of this large roadless area is threatened with logging. *Olympic Mountains Trail Guide*, page 273.

Marymere Falls Trail In the Lake Crescent area. Find the grand fir, the self-guided Nature Trail and the 90-foot-high falls. *Olympic Mountains Trail Guide*, page 33.

Northern Cascades

Damfino Creek A high alpine summer hiking opportunity in a very important wildlife habitat area east of Bellingham and just south of the Canadian border. Use Trail #688 (Boundary

northern goshawk

Way) which is forested for a mile or so before breaking out into high huckleberry country.

Diobsud Creek A very accessible flat trail above a narrow ravine (700 to 900 feet in elevation) in an old-growth forest. Many snag dwelling birds live here. A good fishing spot. About 4 miles north of Marblemount. Use FS Road 1050 to get to Trail #631.

Noisy Creek Need a boat to cross from the north shore of Baker Lake to Trail #609 for very rewarding hike in the ancient forest. Can rent boat and motor for a day from the Baker Lake Lodge - (206) 853-8325.

Baker Lake Nature Trail A self-guided trail and a good introduction to old growth in a small area west of Baker Lake on FS Road 11 near Rocky Creek.

Baker River Trail #606 "Luxurious rain forest." Check on trail conditions. *100 Hikes in the North Cascades*, 1988, page 76. *Trips and Trails, 1*, page 61. *Best Hikes with Children*, page 34.

Kindy Creek A real cathedral forest between Cascade River and Glacier Peak Wilderness that is gravely threatened. The old growth is next to the trail. Use FS Road 1570 from two miles east of Mineral Park picnic area.

Big Beaver Valley In the Ross Lake National Recreational Area of the North Cascades National Park Complex. Enormous cedars, Douglas-fir, hemlock and ghostly silver fir thrive here. Take Highway 20 to Ross Lake Resort and use the Beaver Loop Trail. *100 Hikes in the North Cascades*, 1985, pages 88-89.

Mount Higgins to Myrtle Lake Area Valuable cedars that are seriously threatened can be viewed to the north from Highway 530 about 17 miles east of Arlington. Land closest to river is private, but the slopes are Forest Service land. *100 Hikes in the Glacier Peak Region*, pages 32 and 33.

Barlow Pass One-mile-switchback trail through an ancient forest to a magnificent view. Use Barlow Point Trail #709. FS-ROG, *Best Hikes With Children*, page 78.

Heather Lake Hike through regrowing clearcuts and enter a cathedral forest with behemoth cedars. The trail climbs to subalpine forest and meadow in a valley close to Mount Pilchuck. One mile east of Verlot. *Trips and Trails, 1*, page 93. *Footsore 3*, page 31.

Lake 22 A Research Natural Area, this popular area was set aside in 1947 for study of water, wildlife, and timber in a virgin state. Giant cedar and a series of waterfalls highlight this area. Use Trail #702. Two miles east of Verlot Public Service Center. FS-ROG.

More
Areas

Blanca Lake Lots of spectacular old trees along a steep trail, some Douglas-firs eight feet in diameter. The first 3 miles are outside the wilderness and thus unprotected. Northeast of Index off FS Road 63. Use Trail #1052. *100 Hikes in the Glacier Peak Region*, page 102.

Barclay Lake Low elevation area at base of Baring Mountain about 6 miles east of Index off Highway 2. Use Trail #1055 (a short trail). *Trips and Trails, 1*, page 108. *Footsore 2*, pages 204-206. *Best Hikes With Children*, page 90. *100 Hikes in the Glacier Peak Region*, page 106.

Miller River A spectacular deep valley with huge cedar, hemlock and Douglas-fir. About 10 miles east of Index off Highway 2 to Road 6410. *Footsore 2*, page 210.

Deception Creek This is a fine example of mid-elevation old growth. The trail takes you into the Alpine Lakes Wilderness through virgin forest and by a special creek. Approximately 8 miles east of Skykomish. Use Trail #1059. *100 Hikes in the Alpine Lakes*, page 40.

North Fork Skykomish Can be viewed from a car on either side of the road after passing Troublesome Creek campground. (See West Cady Creek in Northern Cascades section.)

Surprise Creek Gorgeous large cedars are along the first mile of trail outside the wilderness area. Great waterfalls. Use Trail #1060 which enters Alpine Lake Wilderness. About 10 miles east of Skykomish. *100 Hikes in the Alpine lakes*, page 42.

Central Cascades

Sunday Creek Northeast of North Bend. The trail meanders along the south side of North Fork Snoqualmie River valley among giant cedars and into the Alpine Lakes Wilderness. *Footsore 2*, page 111.

Pratt River One needs a boat to cross the river but once across you'll find a magnificent forest. Partially logged early in the century, survivors included Douglas-fir up to nine feet in diameter. Forest Service may permit clearcuts here soon. *100 Hikes in the Alpine Lakes*, page 200. TRIS.

Hester Lake A steep trail into the Alpine Lakes Wilderness that takes you into virgin forests. Use Trail #1105. Northeast of North Bend. *100 Hikes in the Alpine Lakes*, page 212.

Mount Phelps North Bend area. The last contiguous old growth in the North Fork Snoqualmie drainage. Take the North Fork Snoqualmie Road to the Lenox Creek crossing.

Clearwater Wilderness See huge cedar, fir and hemlock complete with hanging moss. Near the Carbon River entrance of Mount Rainier National Park. Use Trails #1176, #1177, #1178.

Lost Creek/Huckleberry Creek Location of an imminent

Forest Service timber sale. A lovely and critical old growth site at the creeks' confluence just north of Mount Rainier National Park. Take Highway 410 to FS Road 73. Use Trail #1182.

Moss Lake Nature Trail A great example of a cedar swamp. (See Camp Sheppard - Snoquera Falls directions in Central Cascades section.)

Goat Creek A short trail along Goat Creek in a setting of ancient trees. Off FS Road 7174 and near Crystal Mountain.

Southern Cascades

More Areas

Dry Creek Mountain goats use this old growth for thermal cover. The area is in a hanging valley and is untouched. About 3 miles southwest of Packwood take FS Road 20 then 2010 to its end, cross country (at your own risk) into the drainage (Trail #125 nearby). The lower trailhead is on Washington Department of Natural Resources land which is scheduled for logging.

High Rock Lovely forests and superb views of Mount Rainier from the High Rock Lookout (one of three remaining fire lookouts). Northwest of Randle, turn south off Highway 706 onto FS 52 about 3 miles west of the Nisqually entrance to Mount Rainier National Park. After 3 miles turn on FS 84 and go 10 miles to trailhead at Towhead Gap. Explore a network of Forest Service roads and trails, such as Teeley Creek Trail #251 referred to in *100 Hikes in the South Cascades and Olympics*, page 92.

Johnson Creek Area A bushwhack scramble along the creek bed — for the hardy and experienced. Southeast of Packwood along FS Road 21. Best old growth is between Glacier Creek and Deception Creek junction. Get a topographic map to show the lay of the land.

golden mantled ground squirrel

Boundary Trail #1 near Elk Pass Pumice from Mount St. Helens lightens the forest and softens the trail. Great huckleberries in season. About 32 miles south of Randle on FS Road 25, or 22 miles north of the junction of FS Road 25 and FS Road 90 (near the Pine Creek Information Center). See Badger Peak description in *100 Hikes in the South Cascades and Olympics*, page 146.

Quartz Creek Big Trees Botanical Area Combine visiting this 60-acre site with a trip to Mount St. Helens. About 18 miles south of Randle. Take FS Road 25, then 26 across the Cispus River to FS 2608.

Buck Creek Wildflowers along with large trees. North of Trout Lake on FS Road 23 toward Mount Adams, then take FS Road 80 then FS Road 031. Use Trail #54. FS-ROG.

Soda Peaks Trail Fortunately this area has been preserved in the Trapper Creek Wilderness. The entire Trail #133 goes through an ancient forest. Stiff climb from Government Springs or a short hike from FS Road 54.

Falls Creek Trail (#152) Climbs through 2 miles of beautiful old growth forest to the top of a three-stage waterfall, while trail #152A follows the creek 1.5 miles through old growth Douglas-fir to the base of the falls. From Carson (38 miles east of Vancouver) take Wind River Highway north to FS 30 and then right on FS 3062 to trailheads.

How to Identify

**Common Conifers
of Western Washington**

These descriptions are only an introduction, to whet your apppetite for tree books. Some incidental facts: Douglas-fir is not a fir tree, which explains the hyphen in its spelling; in fact, its Latin name means false hemlock. Similarly, redcedar and Alaska yellow cedar are not cedars to botanists. On true firs when needles come off they leave a slight depression in the twig Look below to see how Sitka spruce is different.

Douglas-fir: *Pseudotsuga menziesii*

Key Features: cones have 3-pointed bracts between scales; branches end in sharp mahogany-colored tips.
Needles: attached singly on all sides of stems, not patterned, flattened appearance. Lemony smell.
Cones: $1^1/4$"-$4^1/4$" long, oval brown, hang down, 3-pointed bracts between scales.
Bark: mature trees have thick red-brown bark with very deep fissures; young trees have thin grayish bark with sap blisters.

Western Hemlock: *Tsuga heterophylla*

Key Features: top droops like a whip, quantities of tiny cones. Viewed from below the short needles give the canopy a lacy appearance.

Needles: $1/4$"-$3/4$" dark glossy, yellow green at tips of branches, single groove on top of each needle, blunt tip, two distinct lengths of needles in double file on twig.

Cones: $3/4$"-1" oval, light brown, hang from branch, soft scales, very plentiful.

Bark: deeply divided into broad, flat ridges covered by brown scales tinged with red. Young trees have thin dark orange brown bark separated by shallow fissures into narrow flat plates.

Western Redcedar: *Thuja plicata*

Key Features: instead of needles it has scales for leaves, bark is stringy.

Leaves: $1/8$"-$1/4$" long, scales growing in pairs on alternate sides of twigs. Shiny yellow green with a resinous odor.

Cones: $1/2$" light brown, 4-6 pairs of thin leathery scales, cones sit erect but lean back toward the trunk.

Bark: mostly cinnamon, older parts are grey brown from weather, broken into long fibrous strands, usually trunk is heavily buttressed.

Pacific Silver fir: *Abies amabilis* (the Latin means "lovely fir")

How to
Identify

Key Features: bark is ghost gray with white splotches, almost always smooth, bud tips are purplish, spherical and covered with resin. Needles grow perpendicular from the two sides of the twig but from the top lie parallel to it pointing toward the end and concealing the twig.

Needles: ³/₄"-1¹/₄", dark green above with two bands of silvery white below, Needles are notched on the lower branches, pointed on the upper branches.

Cones: 3¹/₂"-6" long, dark purple, sit upright in clusters on upper branches but disintegrate on tree.

Bark: ghost gray with white splotches, smooth or finely grooved with resin blisters.

Grand fir: *Abies grandis.*

Key Features: needles are longer than any other conifer except pine.

Needles: 1" - 2 ¹/₄" long, glossy. On bottom branches needles are two distinct lengths and are on two comblike rows pressed flat as if in a book. Blunt tips.

Cones: 2"-4" yellow green or greenish purple at maturity, seldom seen because stand erect on topmost branches and disintegrate on the tree.

Bark: smooth ashy brown and blotchy when young. Tarred, horney, ashy gray with long sharp ridges divided by shallow narrow fissures when mature.

Noble fir: *Abies procera.*

Key Features: trunk like a tall pillar before reaching branches. Viewed from below, the pattern of branches in the canopy is geometric, almost polygon shaped.
Needles: stiff, crowded, turn up on twig to resemble a brush, pale to bluish green with two whitish lines both top and bottom.
Cones: $4^{1}/_{2}$"-7" long and $2^{1}/_{2}$" thick, barrel-like form with papery bracts bent down over cone scales. Stand on branch.
Bark: ashy brown, ridged into long plates that flake off to show purplish tone under bark.

Sitka spruce: *Picea sitchensis*

Key Features: very sharp stiff needles, bark is scaled. Trunk is straight column above slightly flared base.
Needles: $^{1}/_{2}$"-1" long all around twig, stiff, sharp pointed, light yellow green. When needles come off they leave a little peg on the branch.
Cones: 2"-4" long, buff colored, papery scales with scalloped ends, hang at ends of branches.
Bark: reddish brown with roundish scales.

Additional Information

Mountaineer's List of Ten Essentials

Any time you are hiking, be sure you are prepared for the unexpected. Bring along the following, and hope that you never need them.

Extra clothing	*Fire starter*
Extra food	*First aid kit*
Sunglasses	*Flashlight with extra batteries*
Knife	*Map*
Matches	*Compass*

Public Transportation for Urban Sites

Seattle area
Metro Rider Information - 447-4800

Seward Park - #39 - south on 2nd Avenue
Schmitz Park - #56 or #23 - south on 1st Avenue

Tacoma area
Pierce Country Transit - 1-800-562-8109

Point Defiance - #25 or #27 at 10th and Commerce to Tacoma
Community College, change to #10 to the zoo.

Everett area
Community Transit - 1-800-562-1375

The Wilderness Society Washington State Region
1424 Fourth Ave, # 816, Seattle, WA 98101 (206) 624-6430

Forest and Park Offices

Mount Rainier National Park
Superintendent - Tahoma Wood, Star Route, Ashford, WA 98304
(206) 569-2211
P.O. Box 520, Shelton, WA 98584 (206) 426-8265

North Cascades National Park System Complex
Superintendent - 2015 Highway 20, Sedro Wooley, WA 98284
(206) 856-5700

Olympic National Park
Park Superintendent - 600 East Park Avenue, Port Angeles, WA
98362 (206) 452-4501, or (206) 452-9235 (taped message - 24 hr)

Olympic National Forest
Forest Supervisor - P.O. Box 2288, Olympia, WA 98507
(206) 753-9534

Hoodsport Ranger Station
P.O. Box 68, Hoodsport, WA 98548 (206) 877-5254

Quilcene Ranger Station
Quilcene, WA 98376 (206) 765-3368

Quinault Ranger Station
Quinault, WA 98575 (206) 288-2525

Shelton Ranger Station
P.O. Box 520, Shelton, WA 98584 (206) 426-8265

Soleduck Ranger Station
Star Route 1, P.O. Box 185, Forks, WA 98331 (206) 374-6522

Mount Baker/Snoqualmie National Forest
Forest Supervisor - 1022 First Avenue, Seattle, WA 98104
(206) 442-5400

Darrington Ranger District
Darrington, WA (206) 436-1155

North Bend Ranger District
42404 SE North Bend Way, North Bend, WA 98045
(206) 888-1321

Mount Baker Ranger District
2105 Highway 20, Sedro Wooley, WA 98284 (206) 677-5700

Skykomish Ranger District
P.O. Box 305, Skykomish, WA 98288 (206) 677-2414

White River Ranger District
857 Roosevelt Avenue East, Enumclaw, WA 98022
(206) 825-6585

Verlot Public Service Center - (206) 691-7791

Gifford Pinchot National Forest
Forest Supervisor - 6926 East Fourth Plain Boulevard,
Vancouver, WA 98668 (206) 696-7500, or from Portland
(503) 285-9823

Mount Adams Ranger District
Trout Lake, WA 98650 (509) 395-2501

Mount St. Helens National Volcanic Monument
Amboy, WA 98601 (206) 247-5473

Packwood Ranger District
Packwood, WA 98361 (206) 494-5515

Randle Ranger District - Randle, WA 98377 (206) 497-7565

Wind River Ranger District
Carson, WA 98610 (509) 427-5645

Pine Creek Information Station - (206) 238-5225

Other Parks

Washington State Parks -1-800-562-0990

Federation Forest State Park - Highway 410 (206) 663-2207

Point Defiance Park - Tacoma (206) 591-5337

Bibliography

Arno, Stephen F. and Ramona P. Hammerly. 1977. *Northwest Trees*. Seattle: The Mountaineers.

Burton, Joan. 1988. *Best Hikes With Children In Western Washington and The Cascades*. Seattle: The Mountaineers.

Manning, Harvey. 1988. *Footsore 1*, 3rd ed. Seattle: The Mountaineers.

_____ . 1987. *Footsore 2*, 2nd ed. Seattle: The Mountaineers.

_____ . 1983. *Footsore 3*. Seattle: The Mountaineers.

_____ . 1983. *Footsore 4*. Seattle: The Mountaineers.

Maser, Chris. 1988. *The Redesigned Forest*. San Pedro, California: R. & E. Miles.

Spring, Ira and Harvey Manning. 1978. *50 Hikes In Mount Rainier National Park*, 2nd ed. Seattle: The Mountaineers.

_____ . 1979. *101 Hikes in the North Cascades*. Seattle: The Mountaineers.

_____ . 1985. *100 Hikes in the South Cascades and Olympics*. Seattle: The Mountaineers.

_____. 1988. *100 Hikes in the North Cascades*. Seattle: The Mountaineers.

Spring, Vicky, Ira Spring and Harvey Manning. 1985. *100 Hikes in the Alpine Lakes*. Seattle: The Mountaineers.

Sterling, E.M. 1986. *Trips and Trails, 1*, 3rd ed. Seattle: The Mountaineers.

Stoltmann, Randy. 1987. *Hiking Guide to the Big Trees of Southwestern British Columbia*. Vancouver, British Columbia: Western Canada Wilderness Committee.

Whitney, Stephen R. 1987. *Nature Walks In & Around Seattle*. Seattle: The Mountaineers.

Wood, Robert L. 1984. *Olympic Mountains Trail Guide*, 3rd ed. Seattle: The Mountaineers.

Other Suggested Readings

Ervin, Keith. 1989. *Fragile Majesty*. Seattle: The Mountaineers. Excellent discussion of Northwest old growth forests including economic conflicts, political perspective and potential solutions.

Franklin, Jerry, et al. 1981. *Ecological Characteristics of Old-Growth Douglas-Fir Forests*. Portland, OR: USDA Forest Service, Pacific Northwest Forest and Range Experiment Station General Technical Report PNW-118.

Kelly, David and Gary Braasch. 1988. *Secrets of the Old Growth Forest*. Salt Lake City: Peregrine Smith Books. "Coffee table" book with beautiful, evocative photographs of Northwest old growth and text which serves as good introduction to biology and history of the Northwest's native forests.

Maser, Chris. 1989.· *Forest Primeval*. San Francisco: Sierra Club Books. In this unique "biography" of a beautiful forest in Oregon, Maser traces the growth of the forest from its birth in 988 to its current glory as a much loved ancient forest.

Morrison, Peter. 1988. *Old Growth in the Pacific Northwest, A Status Report*. Washington, DC: The Wilderness Society. A statistical analysis of Forest Service inventories, checked against scientists' definition of old growth.

Norse, Elliott. 1990. *Ancient Forests of the Pacific Northwest*. Washington, DC: Island Press. A comprehensive summary of the latest biological information on old growth forests of the Douglas-fir region, compiled for general readers.

Old Growth Definition Task Group. 1986. *Interim Definitions for Old-Growth Douglas-Fir and Mixed-Conifer Forests in the Pacific Northwest and California*. Portland, OR: USDA Forest Service, Pacific Northwest Research Station Research Note PNW-447.

Olson, Jeffery. 1988. *Pacific Northwest Lumber and Wood Products: An Industry in Transition, National Forests Policies for the Future, Volume 4*. Washington, DC: The Wilderness Society.

The Wilderness Society. 1988. *End of the Ancient Forests*. Washington, DC: The Wilderness Society. Analysis of draft land management plans for 12 national forests of Washington, Oregon and Northern California. If draft plans are adopted, drastic depletion of old-growth forest will occur.

Tim Crosby

We are very grateful for:

The many friends and relatives who, because of their high regard for Stan Dittmar, contributed to The Wilderness Society in Stan's memory for the printing of our guidebook.

The Weyerhaeuser Company Foundation for their generous grant to The Wilderness Society to help with publication of this visitors' guide to old-growth forest sites on public land.

The contribution in memory of Joe and Nell Wilburn, and Donna, Meagan and Mark McDonald.

Ginny Perkins and Luci Goodman for their design and production of the book. Jon Gardescu for illustrations.

Mark Lawler, Rick McGuire, Tim McNulty, Bob Pearson, Charlie Raines, Susan Saul and the many other volunteer leaders in the conservation movement in western Washington who know these forests intimately and contributed generously of their time, knowledge and advice.

David Guren, Mary Darlington, Mark Winey, Susan Olson and many others who either scouted the numerous areas and gave us valuable information or assisted us in other ways.

The staffs in National, State, and City Parks and Forest Service Ranger Districts for valuable information and directions.

The photographers who loaned us their beautiful prints.

Jean Durning and The Wilderness Society staff for their assistance in creating this guide.

The Dittmars: Ann, David, Jane, Tom, Judy and Steve